KABBALAH
PUBLISHING

The
Holy Grail

A Manifesto on the Zohar

Rav Berg

🐛⁹ © 2012 Kabbalah Centre International, Inc.

Kabbalah Publishing is a registered DBA of
The Kabbalah Centre International, Inc.

For further information:

The Kabbalah Centre
155 E. 48th St., New York, NY 10017
1062 S. Robertson Blvd., Los Angeles, CA 90035

1.800.Kabbalah www.kabbalah.com

First Edition, February 2012

Printed in USA

ISBN: 978-1-57189-817-3

Design: HL Design (Hyun Min Lee) www.hldesignco.com

Table of Contents

Chapter 1
The Bridge of No Return 1

Chapter 2
The Revelation Event on Mount Sinai 5

Chapter 3
The Revelation of the Zohar 13

Chapter 4
Who Is Holy? 23

Chapter 5
The Plea of Rav Ashlag 27

Chapter 6
The Garden of Eden Event 31

Chapter 7
The Bombardment of Infinite Thoughts 39

Chapter 8
Why Me? Why Now? 43

Chapter 9
The Channels of Our Senses 49

Chapter 10
Accepting Certainty Consciousness 53

Chapter 11
The Mind-Body Connection 55

Chapter 12
Who Pushes the Buttons? 59

Chapter 13
The Hidden Universe of Activities 65

Chapter 14
The Window to Our Rational 81
Consciousness

Chapter 15
Getting out of Your Own Way 85

Chapter 16

The Cosmic Danger Zones 91

Chapter 17

A Means of Communication 99

Chapter 18

The New Golden Calf 115

Chapter 19

The New Age of Revelation 125

Chapter 1
The Bridge of No Return

It is with deep humility and awesome devotion that I share these few words of introduction to the *Zohar,* the original Holy Grail. It was the dream of Rav Yehuda Ashlag, the founder of The Kabbalah Centre in 1922 and the first contemporary kabbalist, to bring these teachings to the English-speaking world.

In the early 1960s, I was the only English-speaking student of The Kabbalah Centre. Rav Yehuda Brandwein, heir to the legacy of Rav Ashlag, was my teacher. At that time, it was apparent to both Rav Brandwein and me that to disseminate Kabbalah would require setting down, in the simplest language possible, the major doctrines taught by Rav Ashlag.

As a young man who had studied Kabbalah for only three years, I found the responsibility overwhelming. I knew, however, that Kabbalah was my destiny, and this gave me strength. I could not have known, of course, that in 1967, I would be designated as Rav Brandwein's heir apparent or that just one and a half years later, he no longer would be among the living.

Slowly, English volumes of the *Zohar* emerged. But the job of translating and disseminating kabbalistic teachings was monumental, especially since my wife, Karen, and I were also involved in the task of expanding The Centre worldwide.

Those early years were difficult and yet enjoyable ones for Karen and me. We had crossed the bridge of no return and had entered forbidden territory. We were defying the sacred beliefs of the entire world because we believed it to be our destiny to bring the wisdom of Kabbalah and the *Zohar* to layperson and scholar alike. We agreed that this would be a monumental undertaking but also an event in history, so for us, there was no looking back. And now, thanks to the devoted efforts of so many people who have opened their mind to the Holy Grail, the *Zohar* has at last been brought out into the light of day

Chapter 2
The Revelation Event on Mount Sinai

The world was created with parallel universes: The flawless universe, which is known as the Tree of Life reality and the universe of the Tree of Knowledge reality. The Tree of Knowledge universe, however, consists of both good and evil. Humankind has free will to opt for either the good consciousness of sharing and self-judgment (rather than being judgmental of others) or the evil consciousness of this physical, material reality. When we have a positive attitude toward others, we have connected to the good of the Tree of Knowledge universe and have created a bridge to the universe of the Tree of Life, which contains no form of evil or chaos.

Before Adam connected with the evil of the Tree of Knowledge, chaos did not exist. When Adam ate of the forbidden fruit of the Tree of Knowledge, however, he established a connection to chaos. During the following 2400 years, the world tested chaos in its extreme with the ultimate of chaos: Death.

The Revelation event on Mount Sinai was the result of humanity's never-ending experience of chaos and death. God saw no future that would or could change this situation. Therefore, the Scroll, which contained the information and energy to bring about the demise of chaos, was introduced. Was this event, this introduction of the Scroll, a revelation for Jews only? Was it for the purpose of establishing the Jewish people as a nation? Was it for the creation of religion? The kabbalistic response to these questions is a very definite one. No! All nations were privy to this event. It is unconscionable to presume that God would present Himself as the Deity of Beneficence to one nation and not others. To assume that Jews were the favored people of the universe to the exclusion of the other people of God's creation is a corruption.

Yet this assumption has been the popular version of the Revelation at Mount Sinai.

But God, in His infinite compassion toward His creation, again attempted to remove chaos from our midst. Thus was born the second Revelation, the transmission of the Holy Grail—the *Zohar*—to Rav Shimon bar Yochai and his son, Elazar, 2000 years ago in a cave in the remote village of Peki'in in the northern Galilee region of the Holy Land.

Four hundred years before the first Revelation at Mount Sinai, Abraham the Patriarch received the very first work of Kabbalah, known as the *Book of Formation.* This work was so couched in mystery, however, that only a highly elevated individual could understand it. At the first Revelation, the Holy Grail accompanied the presentation of the Scroll, but in oral form only. The written Holy Grail would have to wait for Rav Shimon and a time when the entire world was again thrust into chaos with the destruction of the Second Temple—a time when there was no obvious hope that humankind could bring chaos to an end.

The *Zohar* expounded on the *Book of Formation*. Nonetheless, for reasons that remain a mystery, the *Zohar* was hidden from the world until the year 1279, when it reappeared in Spain through the Kabbalist Rabbi Moshe De Leon. From that moment onward, the Holy Grail has not left the domain of civilization. As stated in the Holy Grail itself, however, the layperson would not understand its messages, mysteries, and secret codes until sometime in the 20th century.

Now the *Zohar*'s prophecy has come true. For the very first time in history, the Holy Grail has become available to the layperson. Of course, the more knowledgeable the student, the higher the degree of comprehension that can be achieved. According to the Holy Grail, chaos and mortality can come to an end, but only with the participation of laypeople around the globe.

Many of the traditional concepts that humankind has accepted will fade away, including the misconceptions involving the first Revelation. The entire world will come to understand that the Holy *Zohar*, which ushered in the second Revelation, was intended for all humankind. Why then were the Israelites designated as the nation to bear the responsibility for the first and second Revelations? Rav Isaac Luria and Rav Ashlag attribute this to an intense Desire to Receive.

The Israelite—and this term includes any individual who behaves in a sharing, tolerant, and sensitive manner—is by definition a person who acts in a Godly manner, with compassion for all of God's created beings. This not only includes a consciousness of human dignity, but also respect for all the other kingdoms: Animal, vegetable, and inanimate.

This was the creation of God, who created with love and compassion. Anyone who fails in this manner does not have the soul of an Israelite. Consequently, states the *Zohar*, all souls, whether in a corporeal body or not, were present at Mount Sinai. And because of this affinity with the deity, the Israelites were capable of receiving the totality of the Lightforce encased within the Scroll. The Revelation of this Lightforce—the first Revelation—brought immortality and the end of chaos to the world.

At the time of the exodus from Egypt, however, some people wanted to convert to become Israelites. They were known as the *erev rav* (literally, "the mixed multitude"). God warned Moses not to embrace and accept these people at this time. Moses did not pay enough attention to this warning. The conditions and environment were too new. While all evidence indicated a pattern of mind control over matter, even to the extent of immortality, these particular souls were bent on advancing and enhancing their stature and egos. And so these *erev rav* overrode all the benefits that the first Revelation had already established for all of humankind.

Moses had returned to the Upper Realm with God to receive the physical Scroll. The purpose for his return was to create a link between the immaterial energy of the first Revelation— which had become infused within the cosmos by virtue of all people of the Earth listening to the Word of God—and our physical realm, where the Lightforce would become encased within a physical Scroll, which could be tapped at any time by all of humankind. The people would then have access themselves to this enormous reservoir of beneficence. They no longer would be in need of any intermediaries to act on their behalf with God.

But these *erev rav* had other plans. Moses, who was to return after spending 40 days with the Creator, did not come back at the appointed time. Just shy of six hours of Moses' scheduled return, the *erev rav* seized upon this opportunity to convince the other Israelites to create a replacement for Moses who would act as the intermediary for them.

Chapter 3
The Revelation of the Zohar

Their plan—to create a living, speaking golden calf—would establish them as the authoritative link to God. In this way, they could manipulate the people, and thereby enhance their egos and position. They knew that the first Revelation would subsequently restore to humankind its right to control its own destiny.

When the golden calf came into being, the plan of the *erev rav* became established within the consciousness of the Israelites. The *erev rav* had brought their well-designed strategy to fruition. The Israelites had fallen from their spiritual, immaterial consciousness of mind over matter and immortality. They had severed their ties with the Lightforce and its spiritual, immaterial dominion over the physical, material reality of existence. The Scroll that Moses had constructed with God was no longer compatible with the consciousness of the Israelite.

Moses shattered the Scroll. And with its shattering was lost humankind's first opportunity since the sin of Adam 2400 years earlier to rid the world of chaos, pain, and suffering. Although Moses returned to the Mount for the second Scroll, the eternal energy to usher in immortality had been lost.

What should have been learned from the golden calf incident is that the temptation to enhance one's ego knows no limitation. These *erev rav* knew the formula for ridding the world of its chaos, a formula that would have permitted the individual to regain full dominion over his destiny. The *erev rav* knew the Israelites would no longer have to depend upon others. His or her life would have rested in his or her own hands. But the *erev rav* did not wish individuals to have such self-determination. Their ambition from the very start was of a perverted nature. They considered

Moses a manipulator and watched constantly for an opportunity to take his place. These selfish, egotistical people were prepared to sacrifice an entire population to achieve fulfillment of their egos. Unfortunately, these very same *erev rav* are *still* provoking the world against the Israelite people.

God warned Moses that the *erev rav* could deliver only destruction, chaos, pain, and suffering to the entire world. One day, God told Moses, when the people have reached a highly spiritual consciousness, these destructive *erev rav* would be absorbed into the positive consciousness of the people, and they (the *erev rav*) would change. But they could and would cause immeasurable harm in the interim. The world would suffer until everyone despaired. Because Moses paid no heed to God's warning, we all suffer to this day.

Thus 1300 years elapsed since the Revelation on Mount Sinai, bringing about further human suffering and the destruction of the First Temple and culminating in the destruction of the Second Temple. This destruction affected everyone and everything in the universe. At that moment, the Holy Grail, or the *Zohar*, made its appearance to Rav Shimon bar Yochai and his son, Elazar. While nothing could duplicate the Lightforce power of the first Scroll, this revelation of the *Zohar* would now provide a second opportunity for humankind to rid the world of chaos. But for the second time in history, corruption and manipulation prevented its power from becoming widespread. The forces of authority again prevailed, concealing the truth about both the first Revelation and the revelation of the *Zohar*.

With the Holy Grail now in written form, humankind nonetheless could take a gigantic step forward. During the first Revelation on Mount Sinai, the Holy Grail had been transmitted orally to Moses. This provided the *erev rav* with the opportunity to smother and choke the existence of this important discipline and teaching. The Holy Grail revealed the Scroll for what it truly is—a coded road map and user's manual on how to live in an environment free of chaos.

The interpretation of the Scroll by the *erev rav* stressed the significance of the deity and ecclesiastical authority, which would establish them as the keepers of the faith. The Holy Grail have shattered this idea. So when the Almighty viewed the Second Temple's destruction and the ensuing misery and death—blood flowed knee-high—He knew that the time had come for the Holy Grail to be written down.

Rav Shimon and his son, Elazar, knew that if knowledge of the impending second Revelation came to the attention of the evil ones in authority, these people would employ every conceivable stratagem to escape being overthrown. Rav Shimon declared in the *Zohar* that the people of the world would be forced to live with their chaos until the ushering in of the Aquarian Era. This meant a delay of 2000 more years, for which Rav Shimon felt broken-hearted because he knew how much pain and suffering that the world would have to endure.

But Rav Shimon was fully aware of how entrenched the greed for power was in the consciousness of the so-called leaders. Moreover, his Divine Revealment indicated that there would be no real change in this leadership and in the characters of the leaders.

Through reincarnation, these leaders would inhabit the universe over and over again, and there was little hope that any real change would take place in them.

The critical moment of change would arrive in conjunction with the Aquarian Age. Then a massive, quiet revolution would occur, and the *erev rav* would be pushed aside to make way for a period of enlightenment and the restoration of authority to the people. The Aquarian influence would be a subtle force permitting the gradual spread of the Holy Grail until it became an integral part of humankind. By the time the corrupt authorities would become aware of what was happening, their frantic and desperate measures to hold on to power would be to no avail.

Why, one might ask, did Rav Shimon see such a harsh future for humankind, a future almost precluding any hope for happiness? Rav Shimon received his Divine Inspiration through his reincarnated soul, which originated from the soul of Moses. He knew that the *erev rav* would have unquestionable power and control over their subjects and that any break from them would take place only after a long period of gradual enlightenment and creeping discontent. Unfortunately for all concerned, the price that humankind would pay was beyond description. But this suffering would be necessary to rid the world of these evil people.

These *erev rav* were and continue to be the underlying cause of hate between people. This was one of the secrets of the *Zohar* that the *erev rav* feared most because they knew that it placed their authority in jeopardy. Were the people to become aware of why hate existed, they would immediately reject these negative authorities. Moreover, if the Holy Grail became widespread, there would be no further need of intermediaries or the deity and its authority. All of humankind would finally achieve that long sought-after goal of eliminating chaos.

The primary factor that fosters anti-Semitism is the denial by the Jew, albeit, the authorities, of the fruits of the Holy Grail. While this denial originated with a few leaders, the blame of chaos has nonetheless been thrust upon the entire Jewish people, including the innocent ones. But anti-Semitism has served the authorities well. God seemed to be oblivious to the people's pleas, so whom else could the people turn to if not to the ecclesiastical authority? Once the *Zohar* made its appearance towards the end of the 13th century, their determination intensified. Their animosity brought on the ensuing 500-year-long Inquisition, which finally came to an end in Mexico in the early 19th century.

The kabbalists who followed the Lurianic period (1543–1572) placed a great deal of significance on the evil efforts of these hateful *erev rav*. Despite their continued success in manipulating the mainstream of humanity, their strength began to wane following the Inquisition. The world, however, was not yet prepared to accept the hateful character of the ecclesiastical authority despite the growing number of kabbalists proclaiming it. When the modern pioneer of kabbalistic discipline, Rav Ashlag, began to produce his writings, he was met with vigorous opposition from the ecclesiastical authorities. When he assured them that he would restrict his teaching to select scholars, however, he was left alone.

Rav Ashlag realized his vision of the Holy Grail becoming available to everyone. Little did the authorities dream that the seeds of Rav Ashlag's efforts were to blossom only 40 years later. Everyone was fully convinced that this newest episode in the history would simply fade into oblivion, as had earlier attempts to bring the Holy Grail to the people.

Chapter 4
Who Is Holy?

When the doors of The Kabbalah Centre were flung open in 1971, many came to drink from the wellspring. Others, however, launched attacks. The Centre was breaking with a 4000-year-old tradition, and this could not be tolerated. It would be unfitting for me to enumerate the many tirades and activities against the dissemination of the *Zohar* in the same book that contains these beautiful teachings themselves. Suffice it to say that the response of those in power was swift, harsh, and widespread. They initiated a campaign to discredit The Centre around the globe.

This attitude, unfortunately, has been common. The suppression of information and scholarship has occurred over and over again in human history. Such suppression was apparent during the time of Rav Shimon bar Yochai and has continued up to this very moment. The authorities excommunicated Maimonides when he made an attempt to codify the various Jewish laws. He and his works were considered blasphemous merely because this codification had never been done before. Both Copernicus and Galileo were forbidden to present ideas that were considered sacrilegious. How the authorities could justify the suppression of such an important document as the *Zohar*, which could benefit all of humankind, remains a mystery. How they could advance the notion that chaos, pain, and suffering must dominate the landscape of humanity because the average person is not "holy enough" to touch, read, or study the content is baffling.

The Holy Grail was presented in oral form on Mount Sinai and in written form by Rav Shimon. No one has ever made an attempt to alter the *Zohar* itself. Even the commentaries, interpretations, and translations have been acceptable to the authorities—with one major exception. Rav Moshe Luzatto's commentaries on the Rav Isaac Luria (the Ari's) interpretation were denounced by the authorities. Rav Luzatto faced excommunication if he did not agree to the withdrawal and destruction of his commentaries. Interestingly, the authorities authorized every work by Rav Luzatto other than those dealing with Kabbalah.

Why has the *Zohar* been singled out as the one teaching that must be denied to the people? Why is its holiness kept from those whose desire is to drink from the wellspring of its beneficence? And who is to determine whether any individual is pure enough to delve into the teachings of the *Zohar*? Who is so holy as to condemn an entire world and decree that it must be forever chained to pain and suffering? Were the 50 million people who perished during World War II bound to this fate?

Chapter 5

The Plea of Rav Ashlag

In 1936, Rav Ashlag warned a black cloud of chaos and catastrophe that was hovering over Europe. He warned of a disaster that would engulf the entire world. He declared that to prevent the impending holocaust, people must embrace the Holy *Zohar*. But his plea was ignored.

Some might doubt that the Holy *Zohar* could have prevented the holocaust in Europe from 1939 through 1945. However, to demonstrate that the words of Rav Ashlag were the words of truth, let us consider Morocco. An event that took place in this small protectorate in North Africa during the German-Italian campaign and General Rommel's drive to capture all of

North Africa and then move on for the final triumphant march against Jerusalem provide clear evidence of the power of the Holy *Zohar* and of the truth of Rav Ashlag's words.

Rommel, the commander of the German armed forces, had invaded Morocco in 1941 because at that time, it had no army of its own and was a protectorate under the protection of the League of Nations. Rommel demanded that the king hand over Morocco's 250,000 Jews. The king refused. And to the amazement of the king, historians, and the Jews themselves, General Rommel bowed his head and said, "Good day."

The German High Final Solution declared that annihilating the Jews took precedence over every need of the army. If there was a shortage of rail cars, for instance, transporting Jews to the death camps would override supplying soldiers with arms, ammunition, or food.

So historians have been puzzled over why Rommel took "no" as an answer from the king of Morocco, especially since the general, by doing so, was acting in direct defiance of

Hitler's Final Solution and since the mighty German war machine could have conquered this little country very easily. This enigmatic event in history still baffles all who hear about it. But to the kabbalist, the answer is simple. It resides in the realm of the metaphysical. For the Jews in Morocco, as well as in other Moslem countries, life did not exist without the Holy *Zohar*. Saturday evening readings were part of their tradition. They never knew a life without the *Zohar*. Only the energy and power of the *Zohar* could achieve the seemingly impossible triumph of mind control over the evil of the physical reality. Because of the *Zohar*, Rommel had no free will to execute his devilish plan of delivering a quarter of a million Jews to their death.

Herein lay the remarkable plea of Rav Ashlag. He knew the *Zohar* could transform the ghastly plan of extermination into a life filled with hope. Indeed, this holy compilation of teachings is replete with tales that demonstrate its incredible power and its status as a producer of miracles and wonders.

Chapter 6
The Garden of Eden Event

The accounts of what reading and scanning the *Zohar* have done for thousands of its students and adherents testify to this document's 4000 years of uniqueness. A discipline that has survived for millennia must have the dynamism to stave off the forces of time. It's almost as if the *Zohar* contains its own immortality formula, which prompts us to ask, "What is so special about this document? What permits it to endure the forces that have for so long sought to bring about its demise?"

To explore the mystery of the *Zohar's* powers, let us reflect upon its own explanation of why it exists. "And Moses said unto Rav Shimon bar Yochai, 'Only through your compendium, the

Zohar, shall humankind taste from the Tree of Life Reality.'" This straightforward and dramatic comment makes it clear that the *Zohar* —and only the *Zohar*—has the ability to elevate humankind to the level of the Tree of Life.

For readers unfamiliar with the concept of the Tree of Life, permit me to briefly discuss the term. As mentioned previously, there are two parallel universes, or realities, that humankind can occupy and relate to. The first is the Tree of Knowledge Reality mentioned in the biblical description of Genesis. The second is the Tree of Life Reality, which no discipline, aside from Kabbalah and the *Zohar*, clearly defines. Many biblical commentaries present the account of what happened to Adam and Eve in the Garden of Eden as historical fact. To the kabbalist, however, the story is rich in information about the secrets of our universe. The Garden of Eden incident, as well as all the other stories in the Bible, is just that—a story. According to Rav Shimon, these stories are a compendium of mystical codes that the *Zohar* deciphers. What the *Zohar* gleans from the discussion between Eve and the Snake is a precise definition of these two realities of our universe.

And the Lord commanded Adam, "Of every tree from the garden you may eat. However, from the Tree of Knowledge of Good and Evil, do not eat thereof, for on the day that you eat from it, you shall surely die." And the Snake said to the woman, "Did the Lord say, you shall not eat of any tree from the garden?" And the woman said to the Snake, "From the fruit of any tree we can eat. From the fruit of the tree in the center of the garden [Tree of Knowledge] God said we shall not eat of it nor touch it, for we shall assuredly die." And the Snake said to the woman, "You assuredly will not die."
(*Genesis* 3:1-4)

On close examination, does this story make any sense at all? The Lord told Adam that if he ate from the Tree of Knowledge, he "would assuredly die." Along comes the Snake and says the Lord is wrong. And after Adam and Eve sinned and ate from the Tree of Knowledge, they did not die. Adam lived to the ripe old age of 930 years. Does the Bible indicate that God was wrong? It is puzzling to me that throughout my years of biblical study, I never raised this glaring question, nor did my colleagues mention it. I cannot recall discussing the issue at all. Once Kabbalah entered my domain of reality, however, I quickly accepted the wisdom of the Holy Grail and Rav Shimon bar Yochai.

The fundamental rule laid down by the author of the *Zohar* was that it is our duty to question everything in the Bible. Why? Because the *Zohar* recognized that the religious authority can be abusive and stretch beyond its permissible boundaries. However, this can come about only when religious inquiry is stifled and ignorance flourishes.

The *Zohar* teaches that Genesis presents the revelation of parallel universes, a notion that has only recently been confirmed by science. It has taken some 2000 years for science to catch up to what Kabbalah has known all along.

The idea of parallel universes is difficult for the layperson to understand. In this Age of Aquarius, however, when things are presented without the complexity of science, we'll be amazed how clear the idea becomes. We can all relate to circumstances that bring out the positive or joyous consciousness within us, and to those other times when we reveal another nature of ourselves that we would rather forget. We all sense these distinct realms of consciousness. They exist side-by-side, although in opposite states of reality.

The *Zohar* states that there are two realms of existence. One is a flawless, non-chaotic realm that is free of pain and suffering. This is known as the Tree of Life reality. If we make contact with this reality and maintain our connection with it, we leave the familiar landscape of chaos, where we are surrounded by the endless and insurmountable problems of life. The chaotic space of existence, which came into being as a result of Adam and Eve, is known as the Tree of Knowledge reality.

When Adam "ate" from the Tree of Life, he drew nourishment from that state of the Lightforce that provides a flawless environment of beneficence, a life free of chaos. Before he connected to the Tree of Knowledge reality, he maintained a consciousness of certainty about the physical state of existence. To achieve the reality of mind over matter, Adam was required to maintain absolute certainty. Were he to falter for even a moment, he could not control the physical realm. It was his certainty that assured him of control over the material realm.

Once Adam had mastered this certainty principle, he was assured of an environment free of pain and suffering. As long as he preserved a bond with the Tree of Life, he was assured of existence within a flawless universe. But when Adam opted for the Tree of Knowledge reality, he severed his connection. The Tree of Knowledge reflected the uncertainty of this physical universe, which is Satan's domain. Here, the law of mind over matter is ineffective. Connecting with the Tree of Knowledge brought chaos, pain, and suffering. It brought mortality as opposed to immortality.

The Lord told Adam not to eat from or associate with the Tree of Knowledge reality as a way of keeping Adam's consciousness at the Tree of Life level. Immortality was Adam's destiny, and certainty and immortality were inextricably bound together. To connect with the Tree of Knowledge reality would bring uncertainty and mortality. So in the Garden of Eden incident, both the Snake and the Lord were correct. The Lord cautioned Adam to tap only the Light of the Tree of Life and thereby ensure immortality without chaos. The Snake proved his point by having Adam eat and not immediately die. However, Adam had now found his way into the temple of doom and would subsequently "assuredly die."

This, then, was the message from Moses to Rav Shimon bar Yochai: The only path back to the Tree of Life Reality is through the Holy Grail, or *Zohar*, which can restore our universe to one of immortality, flawlessness, freedom from chaos, pain, and suffering. Satan wages his eternal battle against the *Zohar* because he does not want to witness humankind's return to the Tree of Life Reality. When the *Zohar* removes chaos from our lives, Satan is vaporized.

According to the *Zohar*, the final victory over all the forces of chaos will occur during the Age of Aquarius. Rav Avraham Azulai, who lived some 400 years ago, taught that the Age of

Aquarius is now; it is the end of the millennium. Now, for the first time in history, the opportunity to wage open battle with the forces that bring chaos into our lives rests with us, the people.

Chapter 7
The Bombardment of Infinite Thoughts

The authorities, who have for more than four millennia kept the Holy Grail inaccessible to humankind, now see their power dissipating. Just as it appears their grip is weakening, they have devised yet another objection to the dissemination of the *Zohar*. They claim that people have gone mad while studying Kabbalah.

This claim is false, as the following illustration will show. I was once an assistant chaplain in a mental hospital that had 5000 residents. One morning, upon entering the dining room, I observed all the patients eating eggs. From that moment on, I stopped eating eggs since it was apparent that if mentally ill people ate eggs, eggs were the cause of mental illness. This is the line of reasoning of those who claim that studying Kabbalah causes madness.

Once the world has drunk from the wellspring of Kabbalah, the face of this Earth will change. Study of the *Zohar* will extract the chance factor from our lives and replace chaos, pain, and suffering with the Tree of Life reality. Even scanning the *Zohar* in Hebrew-Aramaic brings about positive change. More than 400 years ago, long before the modern-day barcode scanner became a fixture in commercial retail outlets, kabbalists recognized the significance of scanning with the eye as a method of fostering a positive level of energy-intelligence. Simply scanning the *Zohar* will create a receptacle within us to receive the awesome power of the Tree of Life.

What do we mean when we refer to a "receptacle within us?" I found this concept difficult to fathom at first. What does the *Zohar* mean when it says that each person can receive the specific dimension of the Lightforce that his or her brain capacity is capable of utilizing? Does the Lightforce recognize the capacity of all the world's six billion inhabitants to capture the dimension destined for him or her? Does some conversation take place between the Lightforce and the recipient? The answer to these questions is yes.

If a human being is unable to absorb a simple electrical current of 220 volts, he or she certainly cannot receive energy as awesome as the Lightforce of God, which is infinitely greater. Therefore, the *Zohar* stresses the importance of the Holy Grail being transmitted by way of a construct in Hebrew-Aramaic. Depending on the individual's capacity to tap the immaterial power of the Lightforce, the *Zohar*'s construct adjusts the flow of the Lightforce from the Tree of Life to allow for its reception by human beings.

When, through the study of the Kabbalah, we achieve an elevated state of consciousness, we begin to realize that everything and everyone communicates unconventionally, without the material of the physical reality. The brain is in a constant state of preparedness to receive the Lightforce. Then why are we not tapping the Lightforce of the Tree of Life? Why are we not picking up the signals that, according to the

Zohar, are constantly available? Because we are under attack by an unceasing bombardment of infinite thoughts. These thoughts disturb us when we want to sleep. When we want to relax after a difficult day, we can't because we are not permitted the luxury of a quiet mind. Satan has successfully brought our environment to a state of polluted energy that constantly infiltrates our inner sanctum, the brain.

To push aside, even for a few moments, the incessant random thoughts that Satan imposes upon us is a monumental task. The battle is too furious. We soon resign ourselves and capitulate to the barrage. But it is only when we realize the extent to which we are being subjected to external manipulation that we can begin to improve our physical and mental well-being. Does the cosmos influence all people in the same way? If not, why not? The answer is simple. The *Zohar* states that the lives of all humankind are programmed by cosmic printouts. How these printouts take on the individual's characteristics is, of course, based on our own lives.

Chapter 8
Why Me? Why Now?

Everything affects everything else. Someone closing an automobile door in New York City can instigate the flapping of a butterfly's wings in China. Because we are now in the Age of Aquarius, dramatic changes are taking place in the way everything relates to everything else. Everything around us is becoming more volatile and confusing. The ways in which we communicate and receive information are experiencing increasing interference. It is through the *Zohar* that we can keep our lines of communication clear and free of chaos. Without tapping into the Tree of Life Reality, however, we remain subject to confusion.

If, indeed, it is that simple, why do we all suffer from such chaos and disorder? If God is concerned about our well-being, why do we suffer at all? When we meet with illness or accidents, we ask, "Why me? And why now?" As we begin to explore the causes of humankind's mishaps and tragedies, let us first examine the *Zohar's* perspective on vulnerability: "A person should take care not to make him- or herself visible to the negative, destroying forces when they swoop down upon the world, not to attract their notice, since they are authorized to destroy whatsoever comes within their view."

What seems to emerge here from the *Zohar* is a startling revelation concerning vulnerability and the existence of security shields. Bilaam, the biblical archenemy of the Israelites and all humankind, searched for the vulnerable point at which he could direct his cosmic (immaterial) attack upon the world. His efforts were to no avail. The Israelites controlled and dissipated the negative energy transmitted by the cosmos. Bilaam's (Satan's) ability to channel this enormous power of devastation was stopped.

The nation of Israelites, as well as all of humankind, came into control at the time of the exodus from Egypt, when the consciousness of the Israelites was raised so that they became aware of the truth regarding the physical reality. They refused to accept inexplicable answers to the chaos pervading the universe. They were not content with half-hearted explanations.

The *Zohar* states that when we raise the questions "Why me?" and "Why now?" the answers lie with the victim. The *Zohar* declares that ignorance of the primary cause of the problem—the lack of a security shield—is at the heart of all mishap and disease. The need to confront the problem of cosmic channeling and cosmic influences cannot be underestimated. The fact remains that when one is stricken with cancer and asks, "Why me?" the question remains unanswered. No one knows the answer. Medical science can relate to cancer or any other illness only after it has made a physical appearance. But the illness began long before its physical manifestation.

It is at this point (before it physically becomes apparent) that our efforts to remove chaos should be the most directed. This is the time of vulnerability when chaos starts its triumphant march toward pain, suffering, and death. Unfortunately for humankind, medicine cannot detect the movement of these unseen, immaterial forces. However, when we weave through the tales and narratives of the *Zohar*, we become aware that our whole environment is engaged in a gigantic cosmic dance.

We know that the Earth's atmosphere is continually bombarded by cosmic rays and cascades of energy coming down from outer space, destroying and creating a rhythmic choreography of cosmic energy. What I am trying to say is that once a lapse in the body's defenses occurs, this allows cells to reproduce into a life-threatening tumor. The victim, no less than the Earth's atmosphere, is then subject to an attack of negativity from the cosmos. It is during these times of vulnerability that illness originates. This same factor determines why one patient lives and another with the same diagnosis and treatment dies. It also determines why one person contracts a disease and another does not. Unchecked, our lives are destined for failure, misfortune, and chaos.

The *Zohar* provides solutions. One is divorcing oneself from the chaotic reality of the Tree of Knowledge of Good and Evil—the familiar realm of physical existence—and beginning to connect to that other reality, the Tree of Life. And reading or scanning the *Zohar* offers protection against the negative influences that constantly bombard us and influence our immediate environment, including our bodies.

Chapter 9
The Channels of Our Senses

Awareness is a weapon for removing vulnerability. We must become aware of the negative intrusions into our lives as part of our effort to remove chaos. When our fortune turns sour, our usual response is to think that we were unlucky. This thinking lulls us into believing that we cannot exercise any control over the uncertainty in our lives. Understanding that what happens in our lives does not depend upon whether we are lucky or not is the first step to achieving freedom from chaos.

Once we conquer our belief that we are helpless, we will have taken a quantum step toward taking control over our lives and over the affairs that affect us. When our consciousness becomes elevated to the point where we are ready to embark upon the most wonderful journey in our lives, then we can step out of the realm of chaos. This idea might seem strange to those familiar with only the western world's mindset. As science broadens its perspective on reality, however, the teachings of the *Zohar* become further substantiated. Indeed, after some 2000 years, science is finally catching up with Kabbalah.

In the kabbalistic view, the channels of our five senses—our ears, eyes, nose, tongue, and hands—are intrinsically dynamic in nature. The kabbalist sees these functions as acting outside of ourselves, reacting to our surroundings and environment and giving us the opportunity to experience the world around us. Our senses are energies, like the brain, that act upon our environment as well as are influenced by it. Abstraction is a crucial feature of kabbalistic teaching. Because we tend to become involved in the structures and phenomena of our physical reality, we cannot take all its features into account. The eye, for example, is can be a powerful healing instrument, as well as a devastating destroyer. Consider how laser technology, which is rapidly overtaking conventional surgical procedures, can penetrate the body without incision or surgery to halt disease. This is the power of light. This is the power of the Lightforce, which creates the power for the eye to penetrate, although we might not be aware of the "incision" that takes place on a metaphysical or immaterial level.

The *Zohar* is replete with narrations concerning the awesome power of both observation and the evil eye. The following is a *Zohar* commentary in Leviticus: "And the high priest shall send the goat away by hand of a man that is E.T." E.T., which means "readiness," contains a hint that there are some men whose ability is the transmission of blessings, for instance, a person with a good eye. Through the priestly eye, blessings and healing become manifested. Other eyes, however, may be adapted for the transmission of negativity and curses. Hence, one should turn aside to avoid a person with an evil eye. The priest was able to recognize such a man because one of his eyes was larger than the other and he had shaggy eyebrows, bluish eyes, and a crooked glance.

What seems to emerge from the *Zohar* is the power of the eye and its ability to attract another person by emitting negative energy. If someone thinks negatively of us, the eye can affect our physical and mental well-being. The energy of a negative eye can extend far and wide and create misfortune in another's life. There are also those who might not intentionally wish us harm but who might project evil. For example, a man who is childless, upon seeing the children of his brother, might mentally focus the lacking thought-energy he experiences upon those children.

I cannot overstress the importance of understanding that immaterial negative energy is constantly assaulting us, so precautions must be taken to create a security shield that will prevent these energies from causing any harm, physically or mentally. The answer, as I have stated previously, lies in one area: The need to connect with the Tree of Life Reality. When we are embraced by the Lightforce of the Tree of Life, negative energies cannot penetrate this shield.

Chapter 10
Accepting Certainty Consciousness

Kabbalah teaches us that before there was the wheel, there was the *idea* of the wheel. Thoughts enable us to create the physical world, and these same thoughts have influence over that which occurs in the cosmos. We understand that the moon governs the tides. We acknowledge that supernovas, black holes, and other phenomena in outer space affect weather and other conditions on Earth. But can we comprehend the ancient kabbalistic belief that the behavior of Earthbound people can exert control over these extraterrestrial influences?

Throughout the millennia, the Light of Kabbalah has flickered. But it could not be extinguished because it has a life of its own, and that life consists of immortality and perpetuity. It is toward this objective that the scanning or reading of the *Zohar* reaches a degree of awesome proportions. The biggest obstacle in the removal of chaos is our inability to accept the awesome idea that we can actually possess a methodology for removing the chaos. Humankind has not accepted that it can achieve mastery over life. Millennia of negative consciousness must be erased. Uncertainty has prevented humankind from ridding the universe of chaos. To move forward, we must accept certainty-consciousness.

It is reassuring to have the Holy Grail, which states that in this Age of Aquarius, the knowledge to achieve certainty-consciousness will become the possession of the people.

Chapter 11
The Mind-Body Connection

Some 400 years ago, Rav Isaac Luria wrote the following on the subject of healing:

> To remove illness, one must take upon him- or herself the bitter conditions of healing for the purpose of grasping and understanding the metaphysical disciplines, which are the secret doctrines of the world. This is the wisdom that has been concealed from the early days of Rav Shimon bar Yochai until now (1572) and as he stated, "Permission shall not be granted concerning its revelation until the final generation that will usher in the Age of Aquarius, which time is

now, through the medium of Rav Isaac
Luria with the assistance of a prophetic
spirit within him."

The Age of Aquarius began in the era of Rav
Isaac Luria. It picked up steam and momentum
over the succeeding centuries, reaching its
zenith in the 20th century, as evidenced by the
technological explosion in the short 100 years
of our current age.

Consciousness obviously plays a major role in
the healing processes of the body. And
obviously, there are specific rules and
guidelines that must be adhered to by the
practitioner. Just exactly what constitutes the
mind, the brain, or the consciousness is a
mystery. The nervous system is the most
complex physical structure in the fabric of
humankind. Its infinite interconnections and
electrical impulses permit us to think, act,
create, and understand who we really are.
Research indicates that the mind participates in
curing sickness, and psychic imbalance is
considered to be the root of all illness.
Unfortunately, René Descartes' 17th century's
philosophy of the strict division between mind

and body led the medical establishment to concentrate on the body machine. Kabbalists have always engaged in what has come to be called the power of mind over matter. They suggest that, far from being a mere participant in the scheme of things, man, utilizing the power of thought, can act as a determinant of both physical and metaphysical activity.

Thought can traverse great distances, can affect people and objects, and is indeed a tangible factor in the world around us. It is no fault of Kabbalah that traditional science does not yet understand that the power of the mind can remove the negative influences of degenerative diseases. According to the wisdom of Kabbalah, the ability of the mind to restore an elderly person to youth lies in whether that person's mind is sufficiently focused with certainty. Without certainty, our minds cannot bring about such profound physical change.

To achieve this kind of mastery over the physical realm requires a transformation of consciousness, namely, a connection with the Tree of Life Reality. The reason that the Tree of Life Reality does not contain any of the chaos that is experienced in our level of reality is that our reality consists of a mixture of good and evil. Good and evil, as defined by the kabbalists, refer to the Desire to Share and the Desire to Receive for the Self Alone.

Once the practitioner has made every effort to remove the Desire to Receive for the Self Alone from his or her consciousness, he or she will have conditioned the consciousness to receive the Lightforce of the flawless universe, which makes no place for the aging or degenerative process.

Certain laws and principles govern this universe. These were designated long before the creation of humankind. We do not determine what the rules are, but according to Kabbalah, we can choose to either prepare ourselves for attachment to the Tree of Life Reality or opt for the Tree of Knowledge Reality.

Chapter 12
Who Pushes the Buttons?

How does the wisdom of Kabbalah view the mystery of the mind? The brain and body are physical substances and are physically connected. Mental or mind functions are not determined by the tidy mechanics of the brain's myriad nerve connections. The operations of the brain in keeping data in an orderly sequence, arranged for relevancy, are startlingly complex. So, too, is the ability of the mind to retrieve pertinent information about past experiences.

The mind, like the most sophisticated computer, can trigger its memory banks to produce a concept. Our conscious minds identify some quality related to the concept.

However, all the conscious mind can do is command and direct a search for the infinite aspects that must go into the processing of all this information. The rational, conscious mind is then placed on a back burner because of its inability to process more than a few instructions or bits of information. Because the physical brain and the rational consciousness are of a very limited nature, humankind has been relegated to a position much lower than a computer that can process fifty million pieces of information a second.

The consciousness we are referring to is that aspect of ourselves that goes far beyond the limitations placed upon us, like on a computer, reaching out beyond the material universe we observe. The computer here in this realm can only process and furnish information based on data inputted by a programmer. Data that either the programmer is unaware of or that is not already stored within the memory bank of the computer is unavailable to the intelligence of the computer.

Intuition, love, loyalty, dreams, illusions, and sensations of peace, joy, and happiness—all concepts unfamiliar to a computer—come into play in our lives every day. Why do these immaterial but integral parts of human behavior surface when they do? Who pushes the buttons?

The kabbalistic perspective offers several important ideas about the origin and essence of the mind-brain interface. These ideas might seem strange at first, but they must be presented. The future practitioner of the Holy Grail must develop a perspective on the awesome power and influence that the subconscious mind has over both the physical brain and the physical realm. A good starting point is the *Zohar*.

Psychiatrists admit that people make use of no more than four percent of their consciousness and that the remainder lies dormant. Scanning the *Zohar* permits us to remedy this deficiency in perceiving the universe and thereby achieve a level of consciousness far beyond the four percent. No other body of knowledge permits humankind to attain this goal of reaching beyond its limited consciousness.

According to the *Zohar*, we fail to achieve freedom from chaos, pain, and suffering because of our limited consciousness. (If our consciousness is not sufficiently strong to overcome the physical reality (the domain of Satan), there is no hope that we can change our relationship to our environment) Consequently, our ability to become part of the Tree of Life reality greatly depends on our minds being free of uncertainty concerning the events that take place in our lives. The forces at work in nature are independent of time, space, and motion, and can best be considered as ongoing states of being. To be somewhat more profound (and possibly more confusing), there is nothing out there or within us but the power of consciousness.

When we are seated at a table in a restaurant, we are subject to the thought-consciousness of the former occupants of those same chairs. When we rent or purchase a new home, the consciousness of the former residents remains within the material of the building itself. In both instances, we must ask whether these former occupants were positive or negative people.

Unseen influences affect our lives and well-being. Objects and thoughts of an unseen nature are not governed by the physical limitations of time, space, and motion. Consequently, the table in the restaurant or the home we inhabit will forever retain the consciousness of the previous occupants. If our consciousness is unaware of these influences, there is very little that we can do to prevent the ill effects, if, indeed, the energy is negative.

Unseen influences also affect our thoughts and behavior without the benefit of our conscious evaluation. The *Zohar* offers us the opportunity to become aware of these unseen influences and to neutralize those forces that penetrate the barriers that have been placed within the universe for our protection. These barriers, whether we call them security shields, immune systems, or ozone layers, can be penetrated when cosmic danger zones are present. The idea that these inanimate entities can affect our health and environment is clearly stated in the *Zohar*. Misfortune and illness are not considered separate and apart from thoughts. Our minds, bodies, thoughts, and environments are inseparable. Therefore, we must treat the thought more than the disease itself. We must treat the entire thought-process that is instrumental in bringing about the disease in the first place. We must also realize that the thoughts of others can cause some form of disease within our own bodies. Fortunately, our state of mind can make ourselves and others well and can speed recovery from illness. We have the power to heal and the power to remain well.

Chapter 13

The Hidden Universe
of Activities

Let us engage in a mental exercise. We're going to make an attempt to quiet our mind for 60 seconds. Sit in a comfortable chair and relax. Now make a concerted effort to keep any thoughts from entering your mind. Could you do it? Although 60 seconds is not a long time, we are likely to fail to ward off our thoughts for even that long. We simply cannot keep our mind fresh and free from bombardment of any thoughts for a mere 60 seconds. This demonstrates the lack of control we have over our familiar rational consciousness. How can we be sure of the decisions we make daily when our thoughts are under constant assault?

If we do not recognize the existence of these unseen, untold thoughts that come at us constantly, whether we are awake or asleep, we will continue to be plagued with chaos. However, when we begin to activate the unconscious mind through the scanning or reading the *Zohar*, a miracle occurs. Because of our connection with the Holy Grail, our unconscious mind is filled with the flawless universe directly from the Tree of Life Reality.

Perhaps one of the most dramatic cases illustrating the power of mind over body, even without a concerted effort being made by the patient, has been reported by Dr. Bruno Klopfer, a researcher involved in the testing of the drug Krebiozen. In 1950, Krebiozen had received sensational national publicity as a cure for cancer. The drug was being tested by the American Medical Association and the United States Food and Drug Administration.

One of Dr. Klopfer's patients had developed advanced lymphatic cancer, a generalized malignancy involving the lymph nodes. The patient was included in an experimental study of Krebiozen. The patient had huge tumor masses throughout his body and was in such desperate physical condition that fluid had to be sapped from his chest every two days.

After one dose of Krebiozen, the patient's tumors disappeared. He even regained enough strength to resume a normal life. But then, when the first published reports of the AMA and FDA claimed that the drug was ineffective, the patient took a dramatic turn for the worse. The tumors returned and the patient once again became bedridden. In a desperate attempt to save him, his physician told him that the reports were false and that double-strength doses of Krebiozen would produce better results. Actually, the injections consisted of sterile water.

The patient again experienced rapid remission, and again the tumor masses melted. Soon he even returned to his hobby of flying. Then the FDA announced its final findings (which appeared in the media as follows: "Tests conclusively show Krebiozen is a worthless drug in the treatment of cancer"), and a few days later, the man died.

How can the placebo effect be explained? Some dismiss the phenomenon by attributing the illness itself to a psychosomatic process. Some say it is a figment of the imagination. However, taken at its root meaning, the word "psychosomatic" means that a medical problem originates and is continuously worsened by a person's own mental or psychological processes. But we cannot disregard any sickness as not being real, simply because its origin is not in the physical realm. Indeed, kabbalistic teachings demonstrate how people can exercise influence over bodily states that were formerly considered not to be subject to conscious control.

Our minds act as healers as well as destroyers. Taking this idea one step further, the kabbalistic worldview suggests that the mind can extend its influence over the entire cosmos. The *Zohar* states that humankind has control over the kingdom of the inanimate. Even cosmic influences, which lie at the heart of all misfortune and illness, can be subject to human control; they can be made to behave in accordance with humankind's directives.

Another aspect of kabbalistic thought is that it seeks to address the prevention of vulnerability. While medical research has not yet come up with adequate explanations of what causes most degenerative diseases, part of any investigation must ultimately address another contributor to disease: Vulnerability. We have all at some time experienced a suppression of our body's natural defenses against disease.

Why does one person become ill and another remain healthy, although both have the same bodily self-healing system? Vulnerability is the kabbalist's explanation. At specific times, the cosmos attacks our natural defense mechanisms. Negative cosmic influences can inhibit the body's immune system. These unseen influences create susceptibility. Kabbalah shows us how to prevent these moments of vulnerability from occurring within our defense systems.

Let us turn for a moment to environmental hazards. The kabbalistic perspective of our universe runs a course similar to that of the new age of quantum mechanics. If we refrain from acting negatively toward nature, we are in harmony with our environment, our physical surroundings, and the cosmos, as well as with our fellow human beings. The survival of our whole civilization depends on whether humankind comes to recognize that human activity strongly influences its whole environment.

But what if others do not feel the necessity to respect and improve our natural and cosmic surroundings? How can I, as an individual, prevent the influence of their negative activity from affecting me? To achieve a dynamic balance with our environment, Kabbalah teachings create the necessary precautionary measures so that we are not vulnerable to negative stimuli.

Our responses to the environment include our participation. We can play an important and active role in restoring a dynamic state of balance. We can assure ourselves that negative energy-intelligences do not invade our space, whether that space is our body or the highway we are driving along. The invader takes on many shapes, the form of an enemy of our physical or mental well-being, an encounter with a drunk driver, or our own dinner table.

To arrive at such a complete picture, the kabbalists developed not only highly refined diagnostic analyses of our cosmos and its environment, but also a unique art of kabbalistic meditation that permits the connection of mental activity with both the physical body and the universe. The brain's 13 billion interconnected cells make it impossible to trace the exact circuits through which consciousness operates. Although physically the brain amounts to only a few pounds of matter, its capacity for knowledge and information processing, along with its unique switching capability, far exceeds the largest computer.

Despite the many scientific advances, a vast and perhaps unbridgeable gulf still exists in our understanding of the relationship between the physical processes of the nervous system and thought-consciousness. While we can investigate certain connections and correlations between physical phenomena and mental processes, the nature of the link between mind and matter remains a mystery impenetrable by scientific inquiry.

There is no question that the complex mechanisms functioning on the atomic and cellular brain levels stagger the imagination. It is highly pretentious to assume that the mystery of thought-consciousness will ever be solved by science's conventional analytical methods. Perhaps, one day, scientists will have models of how impulses create thought, such as a mother's thought of "how wonderful and lovable is my baby."

Many investigators of the brain and nervous system have finally come to realize that there is a quality of the mind-brain interface that transcends the biological. Although contemporary science has discarded the concept of the dualism of body and mind, its investigation of the brain has left it in awe of the mind.

How does the wisdom of Kabbalah view the mystery of the mind? The brain and body are physical substances and are physically connected. Here the medical and psychological sciences find it easy to account for the effect of the mind-brain on the behavior and functions of the body. Most researchers conclude that the mind and all of its functions, such as consciousness and thought, are nothing more than integrated combinations of the brain's physical activities. They give rise to memories, perceptions, and the ability of nerve cells and neurons to change with experience and mechanically execute modes of behavior impressed upon the brain.

These conclusions are, however, mere speculation, for there is no evidence that the source of the mind is in the functioning of the brain cells and nerves. What defies explanation, at least at this point in time, is how the physical input sensed by our nerve receptors converges in the brain to become the subject and substance of thought. Putting this aside for a moment, science, in general, treats the mind as untouchable, even beyond the reach of scientific investigation. The mind, it claims, is simply the product of the mechanical activity of the brain. Scientists talk a lot about the brain but say little, if anything, about the mind. They cannot explain how we can use it more efficiently.

Mental and mind functions are not determined by the tidy, precise mechanics of the brain's myriad nerve connections. Science, consequently, can never conclude that it can account for every activity and phenomenon of mind-consciousness. Herein lies the basis for the failure of psychiatry to resolve our mental health dilemma. Existing scientific indicates that the mind is more than an entity that can be accounted for by the functions of the physical brain.

Despite years of scientific research into memory, the brain's ability to store information and recall it on demand remains mysterious. The memory stores of the brain are filled with information from every experience in life. The operations of the brain in keeping this data in an orderly sequence arranged for relevance are startling in their complexity. So is the remarkable ability of the mind to retain an awareness of events and things that have been experienced and then to retrieve pertinent information about these things from its vast memory bank.

The mind-brain operates on several levels that we do not currently understand. Consider the abstract phenomena of intuition, love, and loyalty. The mind-brain also exhibits unusual states such as dreams, illusions, and sensations of peace, joy, and happiness. And then there is the question of how and why individuals develop unique thinking styles.

The *Zoharic* view suggests that our minds contain the equivalent of a hidden universe of activities. According to kabbalistic teachings, this realm of mind perceives vast ranges of stimuli from many sources. The mind causes whole cascades of involuntary physiological changes. The mind performs complex pattern-recognition tasks and makes decisions that control how much we know about what is going on around us and what courses of action we will pursue.

The mind even directs the events leading up to and including how wealthy or poor we will be. For some, whatever they touch turns to gold. For others, things never seem to go right. The pervasive illusion is that we dictate the scope and direction of mind-conscious awareness.

The reality is that the mind is actually arranged by unseen forces that present to us an already structured situation, which we comprehend in its final, finished version.

From a kabbalistic view of reality, the story of our universe is really one of returning souls. Indeed, no mystery in the long history of our universe is as startling as the universal and repeated behavior of its inhabitants. This subject is so little understood that we need not be astonished at our continued insistence on destroying each other. If we must be astonished, let it be at our inability to unlock the secrets of human behavioral patterns.

Fundamental evolutionary precepts have hardly changed at all throughout history. We have witnessed civilizations weave through the fiber of recorded history, attempting to impose their concept of order. Yet the inevitable process of change, which has become a byword in high technology, makes us wonder how basic life forms still hang on unchanged for so long. In a quickening evolutionary society, people, as well as all other life forms, maintain their desire for the very same things that prior generations had.

Startling breakthroughs that ultimately foster bigger leaps in the advancement of humankind have had very little influence on human thinking. Maintaining the status quo and stability still remain the rule for most species in our universe. Is our mindset really different from that of the Middle Ages? In spite of dramatic environmental change, along with the progress syndrome, have human psychological needs really changed over the centuries? Do we really better ourselves by growing with progress, which continues to become more complex with time?

When we come across information that can bridge the gap between the growth of progress and the lack of change and personal fulfillment, it is really exciting and refreshing. With scientific advancements, we have become aware of internal, immaterial activity that seems to create even more uncertainty. Yet it might be that because of these same scientific advancements, we are becoming so much more enlightened that we now demand to know who or what is the cause of the apparent instability, uncertainty, and chaos in our lives. The influence of the Age of Aquarius will find our civilization preoccupied with information and enlightenment. Although the Holy Grail has been a jealously guarded secret, the time has come for it to reach the masses. We now live in a time of enormous upheaval: A time in which the mores, the traditions, and the answers of the past are all in question.

Our conscious awareness, which plays no role in the initial and final stages of any process, has for too long enslaved us by convincing us that we are indeed in control of our destiny and decisions. The kabbalistic view is that outside forces—whether emanating from our incarnation, a negative activity, or cosmic danger zones—determine our behavior. While we have become accustomed to lives filled with complexity, let us understand that this is a direct result of living within the illusion of our four-percent rational consciousness.

Unconscious processes are far more pervasive than conscious processes. Consequently, the crystal-clear message appears to be that fate, destiny, decisions, and human behavior cannot be understood without taking these unconscious psychological processes into account. The

Zohar, whether our connection with it is made through scanning or reading the text, has the awesome power to not only activate that 96 percent of our unconsciousness, but also to instill in us the energy of certainty that can lead us to fulfillment and a life without chaos.

Some will dismiss the *Zohar* because it offers such simple answers. It is Satan who, over the millennia, has led humankind into the abyss of complexity. We have accepted the idea that physics, mathematics, and other complex sciences belong to the elite. This has hindered the masses from understanding the nature of life and has placed our destinies in the hands of those who "know best." But it's interesting to note that despite its complexity, science has accepted "the uncertainty principle."

It is refreshing when those with an open mind understand that there is a solution to our problems that bypasses the complexities that create uncertainty. Once we recognize that our 96 percent unconsciousness must be cleansed of negativity, we are on the road to resolving the gnawing problems that have plagued humankind since the beginning.

Chapter 14
The Window to Our Rational Consciousness

At this point, I would like to address a question that I am certain many readers have asked: How can scanning the *Zohar* benefit those who do not know Hebrew?

We are all familiar with the bar codes on items in a retail store. When flashed across the scanner, they provide an enormous amount of information that the scanner processes in seconds. The customer's wait is shorter, the checkout clerk no longer has to punch in the prices of each individual item, and the store's inventory is tracked instantaneously. The scanner eliminates pricing errors and saves time, effort, and money.

Similarly, the *Zohar* is replete with instances where scanning by the eye has initiated countless activities that improve the ability of our minds to read and see things around us as they actually are. If an inanimate object such as a bar code scanner can produce such activity, imagine what the human mind can do. The scanner in a department store certainly does not have the potential or the ability to comprehend and understand the myriad aspects that a human mind can process through scanning the *Zohar*.

The eye is the most powerful tool by which we can acquire an understanding of everything around us. As we scan, our eyes, more than our rational consciousness, make the absolute connection with the Tree of Life Reality and therefore permit us to tap into the its awesome, flawless universe. How this works can be understood, as taught in the curriculum of The Kabbalah Centre, by the nature of the five senses.

The eye consists of four colors. The ear contains three sections. The nose has two nostrils. The mouth has only one opening.

From a kabbalistic perspective, if we are to question why this is so, the answer lies in the numerical difference between the four features just mentioned. The reason the eye contains four elements is to indicate that it includes the energy factors of the other three organs: Ear, nose, and mouth. The ear contains three sections to indicate that it also possesses the energy factors of nose and mouth. The nose, having just two nostrils, contains its own energy and also the energy of the mouth. The eye, inclusive of the four dimensions of energy, is more powerful than any of the other senses. The eye is the window to our rational consciousness as well as to our significant subconscious.

Chapter 15
Getting Out of Your Own Way

Science has declared that the human being is nothing more than consciousness. But what about the body? "Oh, that!" says the scientist. "That is placed within the human being so as to act as interference to all things around us." I am not sure whether the scientists truly understand the full implication of what they are saying. Suffice it to say, however, that they recognize that the "me" and the "self" consist chiefly of consciousness.

Our bodies and our rational consciousness are consistently getting in the way of our achieving and fulfilling many of the goals and objectives that we have decided would free our lives of chaos. When my friends experience some form of chaos in their lives, I advise them to get out of their own way. I tell them to place their rational consciousness on a back burner and just permit the Lightforce of the Tree of Life reality to become part of their lives. When they do this, they are amazed to find that the chaos disappears from their lives.

We interfere with the desire of the Creator to share His beneficence with us. How many times have we found ourselves in frustration and disappointment and exclaimed, "God, where are You when I need You most?" The Holy Grail says, "I am right here. If you can only get out of your own way and draw close to the Lightforce, then your frustration and disappointment need not continue to plague you."

This, then, is what we should constantly be aware of when our rational mind raises its head and says, "How stupid can you be, reading-scanning this Holy Grail when you don't understand even one word? Have you ever read the morning newspaper without knowing what you were reading? Would you think of reading a foreign newspaper in a language that you could not understand? So why are you reading this material, which is in a foreign language?"

This line of questioning is something that we have little control over when it pops into our minds. These questions originate with our satanic rational consciousness, and that little devil will never cease trying to infiltrate our minds. He will make every attempt to discourage us from reading-scanning the Holy Grail. Satan knows that the Light drawn toward our true subconscious level of reality—that 96 percent of our consciousness—will remove the darkness, uncertainty, and wrong decision-making that bring about the chaos in our lives.

When our lives seem completely satisfying and structured, we are living under an illusion. The cosmic and environmental chaos is merely waiting for an opportune time to inflict its damage on us and on those around us. Why should we be anxious when there is not even the slightest inkling that something might go wrong? Can we possibly continue to live normal lives under these circumstances and pressures? Must we live our lives bound by the expectation of chaos to come?

The answer is very simple. What the wisdom of Kabbalah is attempting to achieve, through fostering an elevated state of consciousness in us, is awareness that these factors from without are very real but that we can and must take steps to eliminate their presence from our lives. The *Zohar* teaches that the first step is to recognize that our lives are indeed vulnerable to the infinite chaos that lies both within and without.

Before I can even suggest that the Holy Grail is humankind's only means of overcoming chaos, I must repeat that the problem of chaos can and will ultimately disrupt our lives. The *Zohar*'s perspective is that human nature has its origins in satanic consciousness. Satan tells us how we are to observe physical reality. Thus, we do not understand that chaos lurks right around the corner. We cannot avoid it. Yet we proceed, full of blind hope that we might be lucky enough to escape.

This, then, is the goal of the *Zohar*—to raise our consciousness to a new level where human nature no longer exercises control over our thinking process. Changing our nature from being confined within an illusion to being immersed in the true Reality has been the most difficult undertaking. But with the infusion of pure Light-consciousness into the cosmos from the millions of people who now study the *Zohar*, the opportunity for this transformation from our old nature to the new reality has never been more promising.

Chapter 16
The Cosmic Danger Zones

Enlightenment is the cardinal rule for every student of Kabbalah whose objective is to remove Satan and chaos from his or her life. Therefore, it is equally important to address the idea of being either vulnerable or immune to chaos.

There has been a great deal written in recent years about our immune system and why some of us are more vulnerable than others to its breakdown. When we explore the reasons why some people and not others become exposed to the fury of bad luck, we encounter a mystery. The victims of drug, alcohol, and other forms of addiction are generally described as weak-minded people. Kabbalistically speaking,

91

however, people who succumb to drugs are looking for a free adventure without the use of restriction. Medical experts and psychiatrists look at symptoms, wanting to explain states of illness or addiction as they manifest themselves, without exploring the question of why some people are affected and others are not. These experts do not examine the role of cosmic influences and the danger zones that affect people and contribute to the breakdown of their immune systems.

The so-called lucky ones remain immune because their actions have prevented Satan's onslaught, whereas the so-called unlucky ones became vulnerable. If we are to become masters of our destiny, we must understand that an effort is required on our part. We have come to be a society seeking instant relief simply by paying for it. This approach leads us down the road toward disaster.

There are no easy methods for achieving well-being. All spiritual techniques, including the scanning and reading of the Holy Grail, serve as secondary applications toward improving our physical and mental well being. It has been discussed for centuries, and kabbalists agree, that without the Holy Grail, there is little chance that we can maintain our physical and mental well-being. But an additional step must also be taken. We must develop a positive attitude toward both our fellow man and the environment.

With the cosmos filled with negative energy-intelligences created by humankind's negative activities, we find it very difficult to resist and to prevail against this stream of negativity. Meditation techniques, together with the Holy Grail, will go a long way toward helping us overcome these obstacles.

Misfortune, in whatever manner it appears, is the direct result of negative attitudes held during our present or former lifetimes. That we can change the direction of our misfortune is what the study of Kabbalah and the *Zohar* is all about. Embracing negative attitudes is essentially connecting with and embracing Satan. The creation of an affinity with this dark environment prevents any progress in the removal of chaos, whether such chaos appears in the form of ill health, family problems, financial instability, or any other calamities.

There are just two conditions that must be met to guarantee mastery of our lives and destiny. First, our attitude toward our fellow man must be one of humility, something very strongly suggested by the *Zohar*. When Jacob met his brother, Esau, who was determined to kill him, he understood that for him to overcome the essence of Satan embedded in Esau, he must humble himself before his brother. Second, we must don a security shield wherever negative energies prevail within the cosmos, despite the fact that we may boast of wholesome, positive attitudes.

We now have our answer to the enigmatic question of why one person is vulnerable and another is not. Vulnerability is a condition where the future has been shadowed by the past. Vulnerable people are endangered by a genetic "time bomb" passed from a former lifetime to their present one. For every action, there is a similar and opposite reaction. Hurting others results in damage down the line to the perpetrator. Consequently, when opportunity (or misfortune) presents itself again in this lifetime, the practitioner, who is now conditioned to be aware of the importance and significance of his or her treatment of others, can remove that hole in his or her defenses from a prior lifetime by being positive in this one.

The other cause for a breakdown or damage to the immune system is exposure to various negative cosmic danger zones. This was the clue that Abraham the Patriarch alluded to in the *Book of Formation* some 4000 years ago when he named the month of *Tammuz* (July), "Cancer." Couldn't Abraham have had more compassion for the people who are born in that month and not named them Cancerians? He could just as well have referred to that month as "Candy." I am sure there would be no objection on the part of any Cancerian. What Abraham had in mind, however, was the fact that this month is a danger zone for the disease known as cancer. Consequently, it behooves not only Cancerians but all people to maintain a state of happiness and thereby avoid the vulnerability to this dreaded disease. The wisdom of Kabbalah has labeled unhappiness as the antithesis of positivity. When one is unhappy, this indicates a lack of fulfillment and arouses a Desire to Receive for the Self Alone.

This state of consciousness is to be avoided at all costs, particularly during the month of Cancer, for vulnerability originates within this danger zone.

Reading and scanning the Holy Grail will provide the fulfillment that can lead to happiness. With both tools—the Holy Grail and the awareness of the importance of a positive attitude—we no longer will be subject to luckiness or unluckiness. We will become proactive. We will commit ourselves to no longer lie down and die. This is the consciousness that Satan fears most.

Most people who truly believe they are either lucky or unlucky will automatically place their lives in the hands of others. This is precisely what Satan endeavors to achieve, and over the millennia, he has been more or less successful. The Holy Grail, however, is the channel that helps us reinforce our attitude of positivity by allowing us to tap the Lightforce of God, while at the same time removing any chances of us becoming vulnerable to the cosmic danger zones.

The concept of being lucky or unlucky does not conform to the kabbalistic viewpoint. Over the past three millennia, the idea has emerged that humankind is but a pawn in the hands of the Creator. We, in effect, have been relegated to the consciousness of subservience. For this reason, humankind has adopted the idea that assistance or support must come from without. The idea that a rabbi or minister is the only one qualified to intercede or act as an intermediary between us and God has corrupted many religions. It should come as no surprise that the *Zohar* makes it clear that this was never the purpose of Mount Sinai. Our questions concerning luck are the result of the attitude that humankind is lost and rudderless, always in need of assistance or support.

Another example of man being relegated to a position of inferiority is our blind reverence for that modern golem—the computer. We have become so dependent on this machine that we have all but forgotten how to add and subtract. The computer does our programming for us. Today, we find ourselves so enslaved by this machine that we have ceased to think or function as higher human beings. Must we remain at the mercy of these alien creatures?

The *Zohar* is a refreshing relief for those lost in the maze of computer printouts or pacing the forlorn corridors of anxiety. Change is slow in coming, but it is coming. The tenets of Kabbalah have always claimed that humankind must bear responsibility for what happens to itself and its environment. Humankind has been given the awesome power to influence the entire planet and indeed, all of the cosmos.

We do not have to hope that we will be counted among the lucky ones. We can and must do something about it. There is nothing left for us but to read or scan the *Zohar* and be certain that our activities and behavior are grounded in positivity.

Chapter 17
A Means of Communication

The biblical narrative of the Tower of Babel claims that "the whole Earth was of one language and of unity." Language was formed some 2000 years before the creation of Adam, says the *Zohar*. The basic building blocks of this language were the Hebrew letters provided by the biblical text. The purpose of this language was to provide a means of communication with the subconscious of every life form. The Hebrew letters and the words structured by them provide an unlimited vocabulary. These letters and words transcend the limited realm of our consciousness. They can clarify and express more precisely the terms of our thoughts and the observable world around us.

The idea that Hebrew is exclusively for the Jewish people is, from a *Zoharic* viewpoint, a misconception of the language's inherent purpose. The objective of Hebrew is to provide our thought-consciousness with an opportunity to reveal itself. The *Zohar* describes how our thoughts ultimately become manifested in the spoken word. But how are thoughts instantaneously converted into vocal manifestations? The process seems to be completely robotic. Speakers rarely apply any conscious thought to each word that leaves their mouth. They rarely truly think about which word to use or what word will be coming next. Where do these words come from then? They appear to be from a prepared text or cassette that has been established in our mental computer.

To consider Hebrew the language of the Jewish people exclusively is a complete corruption and should be considered a ploy by Satan to prevent the flow of the awesome power of the Lightforce. It is only when we employ the Hebrew language that we can be assured of a proper connection with the Lightforce of the Tree of Life reality.

As explained previously, the cosmos contains a great deal of positivity and negativity, both of which are constantly bombarding our brain and confusing us. Hebrew is the language that will best serve us to bypass this interference. When a reader-scanner of the Holy Grail meditates with the desire to become connected with the Tree of Life Reality, there is much going on between the confusing terrestrial realm and the reality without chaos. What is required then is a cable or channel that will not be subject to the intrusion of outside influences when our thought-consciousness wishes to connect with the flawless universe of Tree of Life.

Hebrew is foreign to the great majority of Earth's inhabitants and this can create an awkward experience for the reader-scanner of the Holy Grail. Nonetheless, once we come to the realization that we have no other choice in our efforts to rid this universe of chaos, we will accept the premise of the Holy Grail that reading-scanning establishes a connection with the Tree of Life Reality. When an individual begins to tap this awesome Lightforce of God, he or she instantaneously experiences the sensation of being surrounded by the warmth of the Lightforce.

We must accept these ideas despite our inability to completely understand the language. We do not refuse to use the telephone simply because we have no idea how the instrument works. We do not hesitate to take medications if our doctor assures us that they will be helpful. If the practitioner of Kabbalah permits the Lightforce to enter his or her very essence of being, the rewards that we have spoken about previously will become a fixture within the landscape of humanity.

The Holy Grail disappeared from the consciousness of humankind for close to six millennia. It should therefore come as no surprise that some dismiss this unique approach to resolving the chaos that has befallen humankind since the sin of Adam. The *Zohar*'s ideas are certainly revolutionary. For the reader-scanner who has never been exposed to its existence, however, this approach of reading-scanning becomes a whole new phenomenon.

We have come so far in the pursuit of the sciences, yet we are no closer to controlling our destinies. What has the universe got to do with my everyday lifestyle? How is the pursuit of understanding the cosmos related to the enhancement of my mental and physical well-being? Now that we have been successful in popularizing science, what impact does science have on my daily life?

It is precisely at this point in time that the wisdom of Kabbalah is arousing interest. Kabbalah raises questions about everything. It zeroes in on the ideas that explain everything from what came before the Big Bang to humankind's power to control the universe and consequently to control our own destiny.

For this reason alone, some people have been fearful of delving into its secrets. They have been afraid of being harmed, worried that they have not been spiritually pure enough to handle its awesome knowledge. In our society, it is still the practice of teachers and parents to shy away from most of the questions raised by the *Zohar*. Many find themselves uncomfortable with the issues raised by Kabbalah. They fear the demands and responsibilities that would be thrust upon them if they discovered that there is the possibility of obtaining control of their lives.

The *Zohar* is the breath of fresh air necessary to revive us from our deep and long slumber. Albert Einstein once stated to an interviewer, "All I want to know are the Lord's thoughts for how He created the world, for the rest are only details." The *Zohar*, in a way that is consistent with everyday observations, embraces the thought and reasoning behind everything, including the details.

Today, when chaos appears to be on the brink of engulfing all of humanity, the steadfast prohibitions against learning the disciplines of Kabbalah remain. In this age of freethinking, when the mind has been permitted to sail beyond its familiar landscape to new frontiers, the ancient taboo still persists. Yet the Holy Grail has finally pierced the iron curtain of irrationalism. Millions of potential practitioners of Kabbalah refuse to be influenced by such outdated, outmoded prohibitions. The scientific theory that the mind can control matter has come to life with Kabbalah. The once-accepted idea that only God can create miracles in our lives is slowly being overturned by the truths of the *Zohar*.

The time is now, according to the famous Kabbalist Rav Avraham Azulai, who lived some 400 years ago. "At the end of the millennium," stated Rav Azulai, "miracles will be as common an occurrence as chaos was, and chaos will become an infrequent event in our lives as miracles were."

What is going to change? Will modern technology take some gigantic step forward and turn existing universal laws around? Will it be some new revolutionary idea that did not exist before? The answer has been before our very eyes for close to 3400 years. I refer to the splitting of the Red Sea event that took place during the exodus. When the Israelites came to the Red Sea with the Egyptians in hot pursuit, they naturally prayed to God to be saved from their pursuers or from drowning in the sea. The Lord's reply to Moses was, "Why are they praying to me?" (*Exodus* 14:15)—a strange reply from the Creator, who has always been depicted as a compassionate, sensitive, and loving God.

Religionists have always explained God's apparent disregard of His creatures by responding, "God, in His mysterious ways, knows what He is doing." Just what did religionists have in mind over the past three millennia when they stated that this was a mystery that only God was privy to? What mystery? The *Zohar* rejects this kind of interference by the religionists by stating that God would never create chaos in our universe. Why? Because the presumption is that God is good. But if this is true—and it is—then where did chaos originate?

The answer, states the *Zohar*, lies in the kabbalistic doctrine known as Bread of Shame. In brief, what this means is that humankind demanded from the Creator that He cease His uninterrupted flow of beneficence. Why? Because humankind felt Bread of Shame, meaning they could not accept the continuing beneficence shared by God without having first earned the right to receive the Divine abundance being showered upon them. This was the reason that humankind was placed in this universe—to choose between right and wrong, to restrict from any activity that would result in treating others with anything less than human dignity.

So it was not God who "in his mysterious ways" gloated over the chaos that humankind had been afflicted with. Rather, He looked on with compassion, knowing that humankind had tied His hands. Then, approximately 2200 years after the sin of Adam, when God saw that humankind was not capable of removing Bread of Shame, He brought the Revelation of Mount Sinai. The Revelation meant revealing the tools and methodology by which man would have a chance to achieve his ultimate objective. This was the first opportunity after Adam failed for humankind to remove chaos from the landscape of the human endeavor.

However, the way the Holy Grail interpreted the event at Mount Sinai was forgotten or met with misinterpretation and corruption. This brought onto the scene the idea of humankind's inability to remove chaos from their environment without the intervention of an ecclesiastic authority. Consequently, when chaos could not be removed, the blame would be placed at the doorstep of God, with the understanding that God knows best. And because we do not understand God, we believe that it is He Who wracks this universe with chaos, pain, and suffering.

I have to admit that having begun to study the Bible at age three, and proceeding through my rabbinical studies and on to post-graduate rabbinical studies at two of the most outstanding institutes of their kind, I never took notice of this obvious discrepancy in the Book of Exodus. Nor did I ever hear my colleagues discuss this contradiction.

"Why are you praying to me?" God said when the Israelites reached the Red Sea and called out in prayer. The response of the Creator to Moses is even more damaging to the whole concept of religion. God said, "Vayis'u," which means literally, "Jump into the sea." One does not have to be a scholar to take notice of these incredible words.

The *Zohar* states that just before the Red Sea incident, the Israelites were provided with complete instructions on how to remove chaos. This technology provided the Israelites and the entire world with the power of mind over matter. This technology can be found in the verses themselves in Exodus 14:19-21. The key is that each of these verses contains exactly 72 letters. I had come across these verses hundreds of times and yet had not noticed this peculiarity until I encountered the *Zohar*. This is what the Holy Grail is all about. It deciphers the otherwise incomprehensible instrument and compendium known as the Bible and gleans from it the truth about the Revelation on Mount Sinai. The purpose of the Mount Sinai event was to provide humankind with the methodology, instructions, and tools by which to eliminate Satan and his chaotic army of destroyers and to subsequently remove pain and suffering from the entire universe.

This, then, was the reason for God's question, "Why are they praying to me?" "Of course," said God to Moses, "I hear the prayers of the Israelites. In fact, I am more pained by the necessity to resist removing the chaos that now confronts the Israelites and to stop sharing My abundance than they feel about their impending doom. However, given that the opportunity for making the effort to assure the removal of chaos in their own lives corresponds to the doctrine of Bread of Shame, why don't the Israelites remember and apply the technology I have already given them to remove this instance of chaos?"

Indeed, while the Israelites stood at the Red Sea, they were provided with the technology of mind over matter and the ability to influence the cosmos, although complete dominion over the physical universe would have to wait until the Revelation event on Mount Sinai. With this information they had been given, the Israelites themselves could split the Red Sea and walk through it. There was, however, a prerequisite to the use of this technology. The Israelites had to exercise certainty. If the consciousness of the Israelites contained even the merest shadow of doubt about whether they could indeed split the sea, they would not succeed. We are told that a man named Nachshon ben Aminadav, upon hearing the words "Jump into the sea," did just that. To the astonishment of the other Israelites, however, the waters did not part. The Israelites began to cry out, "You see! It does not work! The sea is not splitting!"

This uncertainty by the Israelites did not deter Nachshon from his consciousness of certainty. He continued to walk into the sea until the water reached his neck. Only then did the waters part. This miracle clearly drove home the message to the Israelites that certainty was going to play a major role in achieving the ultimate consciousness of mind over matter and thereby relieving the entire universe of its pain and suffering. Without this certainty, humankind, although privileged with the technology to control matter, could not make this technology become manifest within the physical reality.

The Holy Grail contains the information about mind-over-matter consciousness. But for reasons known only to the authors of the Holy Grail, the time for its revelation could come about only now in this Age of Aquarius.

The Revelation on Mount Sinai empowered the people to recapture control over their destiny and thereby remove chaos from their lives. Since the sin of Adam removed the information and technology to empower humankind with the ability to control their own destiny, the unfortunate intervening years leading up to the exodus from Egypt and the Revelation on Mount Sinai would be filled with the familiar landscape of pain and suffering.

The golden calf incident, which came about as a result of the Israelites falling from their consciousness of certainty to a consciousness of uncertainty, pushed humankind into the abyss of chaos, pain, and suffering. Because Moses did not return on time from his encounter with God, they assumed he was dead. In effect, they had forgotten that what had taken place on Mount Sinai was a people's empowerment and that Moses would no longer be their intermediary.

Moses was to return after 40 days. The Israelites miscalculated, and after 39 days and 18 hours, they decided that they needed another intermediary in their dealings with God. These six hours of miscalculation were just what Satan needed. In their uncertainty consciousness, during which the Israelites forgot for a moment the message of Mount Sinai, they chose the golden calf, our modern-day computer, as their intermediary. They no longer were the empowered people.

Chapter 18
The New Golden Calf

In our day, the computer has done for humankind what the golden calf did for the Israelites. It has placed a consciousness-thought within the minds of all people of the world that we are incapable of accomplishing what the computer can accomplish. Humankind has been led to believe that it cannot match the computer in processing hundreds of millions of bits of information per second. Herein lies our mistake. Satan has caused uncertainty about humankind's ability to master the universe. He has led us all to believe that we have no alternative but to believe in the ability of this intermediary, the computer.

Unfortunately, the true message of Mount Sinai would remain unrevealed until the Age of Aquarius. Over the millennia, the people of the world have been denied their God-given ability to far exceed the capacity of even the most high-tech computer that has ever existed or that will ever exist. Satan, in his brilliant performance as the master magician of this universe, has instilled a complete consciousness of uncertainty and inability to comprehend the universe and all that lies around us. We ask the computer for information and are in awe of its ability to gather almost unlimited data, process it, and come up with a fairly reasonable answer. Because of the computer's capacity, we all pay homage to it, while at the same time, we are troubled by our own inability to process such huge amounts of information. This is exactly what Satan hopes for.

Because of the computer's ability to process so much information, the world stands a better chance now of self-annihilation than ever before in history. The reason for this is that the computer, like the golem before it, has convinced humankind that they are not empowered with the ability to rise above matter. How can we even begin to entertain the idea of mind over matter?

Forgetting for a moment that people have structured and programmed the capabilities of computers and that computers follow the instructions of humans, how in the world did we forget that we could not have created something if we did not have that same capability within us? Where could the idea come from if not from an elevated consciousness that obviously cannot completely be transferred to a material computer?

That which we perceive and sense in our conscious mind is the product completed for us just beyond the twilight zone of awareness. The material of awareness has come to us from the realm of the brain that can scan, select, and sort the array of quantum information available from present and past experiences. The database of the brain, therefore, will always consist of information that no computer can ever match.

Within the intangible and metaphysical realm of our minds, fractions of seconds have no meaning. Brain processes take place outside any concept of time. Within the brain, the idea of past, present, and future do not exist. Everything is in the here and now. No computer, regardless of its high-tech ability, can match the thoroughness or speed of the human mental computer.

Humankind places too much emphasis on the rational conscious level of the brain. To multiply 746,234 by 468,888 and come up with an instant answer would be an almost impossible feat for our rational consciousness, but a calculator can perform this task in a matter of seconds. We forget, however, that there is the 96-percent feature in our brain. This metaphysical or unconscious level can accomplish infinitely greater processing than the most sophisticated computer available. We cannot fully comprehend the conscious experience without recognizing the input of the unconscious metaphysical processes.

The new cognitive models of the brain, as understood by science, show how little influence our conscious mind exerts over our physical senses and behavior. The conscious mind does not play the dominant role we once thought it did. It follows, then, that our observations with our physical senses are so limited that it is foolish to place any credibility on their conclusions.

So why does science continue traveling down a path that must end with inconclusiveness? One becomes appalled when reading of scientific "discoveries" in newspapers and scientific journals to find that reports and articles conclude with statements such as, "These findings still remain inconclusive, unsupported by hard evidence."

Once we recognize that the four-percent rational consciousness is not the origin of human behavior or, for that matter, anything that ultimately becomes manifested in the physical realm, we will have freed ourselves from the illusion that the mind is incapable of processing information that we assume is beyond our capability. The question remains: If the 96-percent immaterial, unconscious aspect of our minds can indeed process an infinite number of bits of information, why are we faced with so much indecision and uncertainty?

Why can't the rational mind (the four percent) connect with our unconscious, infinite ability (the 96 percent) and thus provide humankind with the benefits and conclusions that emerge from the unconscious mind?

Our rational minds cannot process as much information as the computer—and certainly not as quickly—because of the bombardment of information that we are subject to, as I mentioned before. As a result of this bombardment, our minds are in a state of confusion, and the true capabilities of our mental computer are burdened under a heavy load of negative baggage from our present or former lifetimes.

What emerges from the foregoing is that humankind suffers from two basic modes of chaos. First, our rational mind is disconnected from our unconscious mind. We therefore operate with very little of our potential. A bridge of some sort is needed so that we can avail ourselves of the full capacity of our mind-computer. Secondly, the totality of our mind is subject to negative information, which creeps into our mental computer and interferes with our ability to reach conclusive or clear direction.

This is where the Holy Grail comes into play. Reading-scanning the *Zohar* affords us the opportunity to bridge our physical-rational consciousness with the metaphysical-immaterial consciousness. More importantly, the Holy Grail serves as a filtering agent, removing chaotic bits of information from the mind. By employing the doctrine that darkness or chaos cannot coexist with the flawless universe of the Tree of Life, to which the Holy Grail permits access, the Lightforce of Tree of Life will automatically remove and vaporize negative or chaotic bits of information.

Werner Heisenberg, author of *The Uncertainty Principle* and inventor of matrix mechanics, the first version of quantum mechanics, produced his own language using sets of conceptual tools to describe reality. Since everyone's mind is unique, however, how can any one person's description of reality be accepted? But such acceptance is easy for us, for we have abdicated the responsibility to do things and to think for ourselves. We have preferred to depend on intermediaries who "know" what is good for us, so why should we think that things would be better? For the past six millennia, humankind's lot in this universe hasn't really improved, aside from what appear to be physical conveniences that have also brought with them the problems of a so-called enlightened society.

Heisenberg believed that all physical reality, which includes subatomic materials, changes at the whim of the human observer. When deeply understood, this 20th century statement is frightening. What Heisenberg was stating, in effect, was that each person can influence others. Every person can bombard every other person with negative thoughts.

Heisenberg said that ever since quantum mechanics was discovered, the quantum reality implies that we must take virtually the whole universe into account when seeking the true cause of any physical event. We might as well say farewell to physics as it has been practiced for the past several hundred years. We can say goodbye to the hope of finding the cause of chaos in this universe. To take the entire universe into account is too much, even for a computer. And to state it simply, who is knowledgeable in every facet of the entire universe and therefore qualified to program the most advanced computer with this universal knowledge? Is it any wonder that the world cannot extricate itself from chaos?

The *Zohar* embraces the thought and reasoning behind everything, including precise details. The ultimate theory in the *Zohar* is consistent with everyday observations. Science has finally caught up with this 4000-year-old tradition.

The Holy Grail brings to an end a long chapter in the history of humanity's intellectual struggle to understand the universe. It also revolutionizes our consciousness, thus enhancing the quality of our daily lives. The Holy Grail provides the means for time-travel by eliminating the limitations that time places upon us. With it, we could all see the future, the past, and the present, all as one. This time machine, which is included and provided by the Holy Grail, can readily take us from our disordered, disoriented present to an orderly arranged future.

Time is moving at an ever-increasing speed. In an amazingly short span of time, we have gone from horse and buggy to space travel. The communications industries have leapt ahead, introducing computers, television, video, and video-conferencing. To what can we attribute this phenomenal change? Why is it occurring now? According to the *Zohar*, "all the celestial treasures and hidden mysteries that were not revealed to succeeding generations, from the time of the Holy Grail's first appearance 2000 years ago, will be revealed in the Age of Aquarius" (*Zohar II*, 81b).

The new age will provide us with a new comprehension of our familiar universe as well as that which lies beyond the range of physical observation in the realm of the immaterial, the metaphysical, and the non-space domains.

Chapter 19
The New Age of Revelation

Today, we are witnessing the beginning of a new age of revelation. Today, more than at any other time in history, the Lightforce is demanding to be revealed. This is the secret of the Age of Aquarius. Until now, humankind's developing consciousness has been left to humankind alone. This endeavor has failed dismally: For six millennia, the minds of men have produced revelations and innovations, but nothing that could eradicate the ills of the world.

As the 20th century approached, consciousness broke out in a way unheard of previously. According to the Holy Grail, we can attribute this to the Lightforce of God, Which had remained on the sidelines to permit humankind the opportunity to develop and reach a higher awareness. But observing humankind's failure to do so, the cosmic force known as the Age of Aquarius beckoned and permitted the Lightforce of God to enter and fulfill God's desire to share His full beneficence.

The doctrine known as Bread of Shame tells us that humankind felt ashamed at the one-sidedness of their relationship with the Creator. It was the Creator's wish and sole purpose to bestow abundance on His creations. His creations could partake of His abundance only to the degree that their sense of shame would allow them. The Creator, in accordance with the kabbalistic doctrine of "no coercion in spirituality"—even in abundance, caused the souls of humankind to undergo a contraction to allow them to refuse to receive without having earned it. This caused a separation between the Creator and the emanated ones, or souls.

This separation in turn forced the Creator to refrain and restrict His beneficence from humankind until they had earned it. The coming of the Age of Aquarius has infused humankind's consciousness, and the incredible

20th century appeared upon the stage of history. The Age of Aquarius can be likened to the Revelation on Mount Sinai. Revelation—the connection between the naked energy of the Lightforce and humankind—means the Lightforce is revealed without the usual protective elements that conceal and dilute its awesome power. Total Revelation would be similar to the disappearance of the ozone layer, which diminishes the brilliance and heat of the sun but also protects the Earth's environment.

The Revelation on Mount Sinai revealed the Lightforce completely, without any barriers that might prevent the full impact of the Lightforce from reaching us. The elements that consist of the material limitations that brought about chaos could not coexist with the Lightforce once the Lightforce revealed itself in its full brilliance. Darkness cannot coexist with light. The ultimate manifestation of chaos—death of the physical body—came to an end because the Lightforce had vaporized the darkness connected to the body.

Why is chaos from a kabbalistic perspective said to be illusionary? Because anything that is not eternal is illusionary. Anything that is not eternal lacks substance and therefore is not real. Because such elements are illusionary, we have chaos in our lives. All chaos, including death, ceased to exist at the Revelation on Mount Sinai. Although immortality has become almost a reality at the present time, for many millennia, death was an absolute reality. Because the *Zohar* has defined the Revelation as the removal of mortality, we can now understand that death, too, is illusionary.

With the removal of the illusionary, corporeal realm of existence, the impediments cease to exist. At the time of Revelation, the idea of the speed of light had no reference. Movement is instantaneous once we consciously decide where we want to be. This idea can be verified by merely inserting into our consciousness the idea that, for instance, we would like to be at a place where we spent a vacation. Being there becomes in our minds an instant reality. Space, as we know it, has no place once our illusionary, physical realm disappears. Time ceases to exist. Past, future, and present become one.

The *Zohar* states that the generation of the exodus saw all future generations of humankind, right up the Age of Aquarius. This reveals that events can operate not only from the present into the future, but also from the future to the present. The Lightforce is our time machine, our entrance to the Higher Worlds. We should focus our attention accordingly.

Only the Lightforce is capable of removing the illusion and limitation of corporeal reality, revealing a cosmic model that is, was, and always will be full of certainty. The awesome power of the Lightforce, to which we are connected by the *Zohar*, is the ultimate connection. During the Age of Aquarius, humankind can again connect with the Lightforce. Through this connection, we can achieve an altered state of consciousness in which past and future are here now, where our youth is again upon us, where we will benefit from the Fountain of Youth, where death has been terminated.

Through the study of Kabbalah, these principles are accessible to all. We can connect with the world of certainty and order, and leave behind the illusionary world of chaos and disorder. With frightening clarity, the Holy *Zohar* leads us to forms of great simplicity and beauty that we have never before encountered.

We have an orderly universe around us. Before we can access this universe, however, we must rid ourselves of the belief that we are helpless human beings aboard a rudderless ship in a stormy sea. We must assure ourselves that we will master the course of our lives. The Holy *Zohar* restores the mind to a central position in our universe. Through reading and scanning the *Zohar*, we tunnel through space and time. We travel at the speed of light toward the Revelation and connect with it, and the Tree of Life reality unfolds before our eyes.

Coming to grips with these seemingly outlandish notions taxes the imagination. And yet history has shown that the truth always turns out to be more wonderful than anything we can imagine. The Holy *Zohar*, our Holy Grail, leads us to a state of mind in which we are connected with the infinite continuum, where time, space, and motion are unified, where past, present, and future are entwined, where everyone and everything is interconnected, where then is now, and now is beautiful.

Other Books by Rav Berg

Days of Power Vol. 1

Days of Power Vol. 2

Education of a Kabbalist

Energy of the Hebrew Letters

Immortality

Kabbalistic Astrology

The Kabbalah Method

The Kabbalah Connection

Kabbalah for the Layman

Miracles, Mysteries & Prayer Vol. 1

Miracles, Mysteries & Prayer Vol. 2

Nano

Navigating the Universe

The Power of One

The Star Connection

Taming Chaos

Wheels of a Soul

The *Zohar*

Composed more than 2,000 years ago, the 23-volume *Zohar* is a commentary on biblical and spiritual matters written in the form of conversations among teachers. It was given to all humankind by the Creator to bring us protection, to connect us with the Creator's Light, and ultimately to fulfill our birthright of transformation. The *Zohar* is an effective tool for achieving our purpose in life.

More than eighty years ago, when The Kabbalah Centre was founded, the *Zohar* had virtually disappeared from the world. Today, all this has changed. Through the editorial efforts of Michael Berg, the *Zohar* is available in the original Aramaic language and for the first time in English with commentary.

We teach Kabbalah, not as a scholarly study but as a way of creating a better life and a better world.

Who We Are:

The Kabbalah Centre is a non-profit organization leading the way in making Kabbalah understandable and relevant in everyday life. The Centre was founded by Rav Yehuda Ashlag in 1922, and now spans the globe with brick-and-mortar locations in more than 40 cities as well as an extensive online presence. Our funds are used in the research and development of new methods to make Kabbalah accessible and understandable.

What We Do:

We translate and publish kabbalistic texts, develop courses, classes, online lectures, books, audio products; provide one-on-one instruction, and host local and global energy connections and tours. As the principles of Kabbalah emphasize sharing, we provide a volunteer program so that our students can participate in charitable initiatives.

How We Teach:

For every student, there is a teacher.

Our goal is to ensure that each student is supported in his or her study. Teachers and mentors are part of the educational infrastructure. Many of our classes take place in physical locations around the world; however, with today's increasing need and desire for alternative ways of learning, The Kabbalah Centre also offers instruction by phone, in study groups, and online through Webinars and classes, as well as self-directed study in audio format.

Student Support:

Because Kabbalah can be a deep and constant study, it is helpful to have a teacher on the journey to acquiring wisdom and growth. With more than 300 teachers internationally serving over 100 locations, in 20 languages, there is always a teacher for every student and an answer for every question. All Student Support instructors have studied Kabbalah under the supervision of Kabbalist Rav Berg. For more information call 1 800 Kabbalah.

Kabbalah University (ukabbalah.com):

Kabbalah University (ukabbalah.com) is an online university providing lectures, courses, and events in English and Spanish. This is an important link for students in the United States and around the globe, who want to study Kabbalah but don't have access to a Kabbalah